D1512557

WHAT YOUR
RABBIT NEEDS

— By Betsy Sikora Siino —

A Dorling Kindersley Book

Long, silky ear

Oily fur helps keep
the rabbit dry

Eye

Nose

Sharp front
teeth

Fluffy tail
is called a
scut

Long hind leg
for jumping

Sharp nails for
burrowing

Short front leg for balance

WHAT YOUR RABBIT NEEDS

	Less	1	2	3	4	5	More
Time commitment					✓		
Exercise				✓			
Play time					✓		
Space requirements			✓				
Grooming (depending on breed)					✓		
Feeding				✓			
Cleaning up				✓			
Life span					✓		
Good with kids 5 to 10				✓			
Good with kids 10 and over					✓		

CONTENTS

Foreword by Bruce Fogle, DVM

There is no need for me to tell you, since I am sure you know already, that the rabbit is growing in popularity faster than any other type of pet animal. In some parts of North America and Northern Europe she has become almost as popular as dogs and cats. And it all started when rabbits moved out of the hutch and into the living room.

Meeting Muffi

As a practicing veterinarian I have always seen rabbits, but virtually all of them lived in straw-filled hutches in gardens. Around twenty years ago I started to see apartment rabbits – bunnies kept indoors. Let me tell you about the first apartment rabbit I met, Muffi Yamazaki. When I rang the doorbell, Muffi was there to greet me.

Rabbits are not garden ornaments. They are sociable animals, and do best when we make them part of our lives.

While I spent time with the human members of the Yamazaki family, Muffi twitched her nose, investigated my shoes, hopped around the dining room, visited the kitchen to use her litter box and returned. She was part of the family.

Muffi is but one example of the pleasure of keeping a rabbit as a companion. Shortly after meeting Muffi, one of my clients brought her cat in because it had been in a fight. I asked with whom, and was told, "The buck rabbit in our neighbor's garden." I was on a fast learning curve, discovering facts I had not been taught in veterinary school.

THE MORE WE KNOW, THE BETTER

Since that time, the veterinary profession's ability to attend to the needs of rabbits and their owners has increased enormously. Rabbit medicine, rabbit surgery, rabbit behavior, all these are standard components of continuing education meetings for vets. Vaccines are readily available to help prevent infectious disease and drugs are newly licensed for use in pet rabbits. The progression of knowledge has been outstanding.

There are some other things you should know about rabbits: They need to chew in order to stay healthy, and will chew up anything they can get their ever-growing teeth on. That means you'll need to protect your rabbit from the dangers of your house (such as electrical cords and houseplants), and your house from the dangers of your rabbit.

Rabbits are highly sociable and more opinionated than unsuspecting people think they are. They thrive on companionship and deteriorate in isolation. They are not at their best living outside in the garden. We should respect their psychological as well as physical and environmental needs. We must protect them from the emotional isolation of the solitary hutch as well as from the dangers posed by the natural predators around us, and also the predators we keep as pets.

Getting off to the right start is the best preventive medicine I can suggest. This little book will help set you on a proper course towards what I hope will be a fruitful, rewarding relationship with your rabbit.

MORE THAN JUST A PAIR OF EARS

Long before the dawn of the first millennium, sometime around 600 B.C., the long-eared, soft-furred animal we call the rabbit was domesticated. This fateful step was orchestrated in various regions of Europe and Africa. The sweet-faced animal upon whom those early domesticators set their sights had changed very little in terms of appearance and habits since her first ancestors roamed the landscape thousands, perhaps even millions, of years before.

Unfortunately for the rabbit, domestication was not to make this adorable fuzzy creature a family pet, but for the meat and fur she could provide her domesticators. It was not until the eighteenth century that the rabbit would charm her keepers into recognizing her qualities as a pet. From then on, an increasing number of people, primarily in Europe and the United States, have chosen rabbits as companions and breed them specifically for that purpose – in a wide variety of breeds, coat colors, patterns, and textures.

Today's domestic rabbits inherited their curious natures, intelligent minds, and complex social structures from wild ancestors who were as adorable as they were savvy in the art of survival. Wild rabbits are profoundly social animals who live in family groups, or colonies, typically in underground networks of tunnels, burrows, and nests called warrens. In the name of survival, each colony operates under a strict social code. Each member of the clan knows his or her place, and the group is headed by a dominant male and a dominant female.

Wild rabbits reproduce at staggering rates; communicate through a combination of body postures, actions, and vocalizations; and spend their days foraging for food and protecting themselves and their families from predators, typically within well-defined territories. Rabbit owners are wise to look to the habits and behaviors of their pets' wild cousins for clues as to how their domestic rabbits can be housed and handled most comfortably.

To best understand your pet rabbit, you must acknowledge and respect the fact that she is first and foremost a prey animal. Ever wary to the threat of predators (including humans), the rabbit relies on a combination of senses, wit, and physical responses to survive. Her long hind legs and powerful hindquarters propel her forward quickly and efficiently, while her keen senses of hearing (facilitated by those signature ears) and smell (facilitated by the ever-twitching nose) keep her always on alert to potential danger.

With a potential life span of eight to ten years, rabbits thrive best when offered proper diet and housing, ample social interaction with their families, stimulating activity outside of their cages, and plenty of safe material on which they may chew. Rabbits are world-champion chewers, yet they are not rodents. A variation in their dental structures classifies rabbits as lagomorphs.

Live with a rabbit awhile and gain her trust, and you come to see her not as the meek, timid, wary little animal that her stereotyped image might convey, but as a pet who is quite affectionate, active, trainable (even litter box trainable), obstinate, fun-loving, and mischievous. The rabbit is an engaging, quiet, very clean animal who can fit quite nicely into virtually any family – even those, under proper management, with children and other pets.

LET'S GO SHOPPING

One of the kindest – and wisest – steps you can take is to prepare for your rabbit's arrival long before she joins your family. You must do your homework ahead of time. This applies not only to deciding whether a rabbit is the right pet for you (and if you are the right caretaker for a rabbit), but also figuring out just what your pet will require for a comfortable and fulfilling life in your home. A rabbit who is introduced to a comfortable, well-appointed cage as soon as she comes into her new family will settle into her new life far more quickly and easily than one whose homecoming is disorganized and chaotic.

Rabbits are very clean and fastidious animals, rather set in their ways and opinionated about how a rabbit should spend her days. To keep your rabbit living in the style to which her species has been accustomed for thousands of years, you are wise to get all the components of your rabbit dream house ahead of time. After all, you don't want to have to run out shopping just when you should be admiring your new bunny. The ingredients of a happy rabbit dream home include the cage or hutch and accessories:

Ceramic dishes are a good choice; they are easy to keep clean.

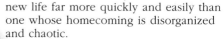

- Feeding dishes
- Water bottle
- Cozy bed or nest box (a comfortable sanctuary in which the rabbit may sleep and hide, preferably made of a chew-proof material)
- Hay rack
- Safe bedding material

A hanging water bottle means hay, bedding, and dirt won't collect in your pet's water.

○ Litter box (get one for inside the cage and one for when your bunny is out and about), litter, and scoop

○ A sturdy rabbit carrier to take your pet home and to bring her to the veterinarian or on family trips in the future.

INSIDE THE HOUSE

The most humane way to keep your rabbit is indoors, with you, and that is what I will be concentrating on here. An outdoor arrangement poses too much danger to a rabbit, exposing her to predators (and physically debilitating fear, even if her cage is safe from attack), disease, bad weather, and less time with you – and that means less bonding and more loneliness and boredom for these smart, social critters. Regard your rabbit as family, and treat her accordingly.

MORE TO BUY

While housing is of paramount importance to the health and well-being of a pet rabbit, proper care of the bunny involves far more than simply setting up a cage, installing the rabbit inside and making sure her food bowl is full. We are speaking here of a very intelligent animal who requires exercise and attention every day, so you must not ignore your pet's need for fun and entertainment.

Your rabbit needs plenty of social interaction and activity, which means she should spend part of her time outside her cage. By the same token, her time spent in her cage should be stimulating, comforting, and enjoyable. You don't want your pet to feel as if she has been relegated to prison every time she returns to her home. To keep life interesting for your rabbit, you can supply her with certain items that, inside or outside of her cage, will help to keep her entertained, healthy, and safe. You can get some of these things before your bunny comes home, but once you get to know your particular rabbit's personality and her individual likes and dislikes you'll want to do some more shopping.

TOYS AND CHEWS

On the entertainment front, supply your pet with a variety of safe toys and things to chew on. Remember, rabbits need to chew both for psychological satisfaction and dental health. You must make sure your pet has plenty of things that are safe to chew on, because if you don't she will set out in search of her own chew materials – and that could prove detrimental to both your bunny's health and the condition of your home. Safe chew items include wooden chewing blocks designed specifically for rabbits, cardboard tubes, and a variety of chew toys available at well-stocked pet supply stores.

Some toys can be left for your bunny to play with, and some will need your supervision. Anything that can't be safely chewed should be put away when you're not playing together.

FOOD AND HAY

Hay – preferably hay harvested and processed especially for rabbits – is another chewing material that will benefit the rabbit internally as well as dentally. Buy an ample supply of both hay and commercially available pelleted rabbit food, but not too much. Rabbit food can spoil quickly, so avoid the impulse to stock up at the warehouse store.

Hay in a hay rack

HARNESS AND LEASH

You might also consider buying a harness and leash for your pet, because many rabbits can be trained to hop on a leash, or at least to join their owners outdoors while safely controlled in this manner.

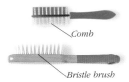

Comb

Bristle brush

GROOMING SUPPLIES

It's never too early to buy your pet's grooming supplies, either, including a brush, comb, and nail clippers.

MORE HELP

Of course, now is also the time to buy a book on rabbit care, and to check out the local veterinarians to find one who specializes in the care of rabbits (not all veterinarians do). All of this will help ensure that you are prepared to offer your new pet the best care possible from the very beginning.

A RABBIT DREAM HOME

Your new rabbit's proper dream home should include a place to eat, a place to sleep, a place to play and a place to eliminate. A cage alone will not suffice. Think back to what you know about a wild rabbit's natural living situation, and there you will find your most important clues to what your pet needs. Wild rabbits live in networks of underground tunnels and dens, providing them not only with ample space in which to move around, but also with various "rooms" for specific purposes. This means you must provide your pet with a spacious, safe cage or enclosure with plenty of room for each of the things she will do in her cage.

The foundation of your pet rabbit's home is the cage, preferably one of those designed specifically for rabbits,. These are available in a variety of styles and sizes at most pet supply stores. Because rabbits vary dramatically in size by breed and individual, there is no standard cage size that is appropriate for every bunny. In addition to being roomy enough for the various rabbit accessories and "rooms," the cage must be large enough to permit the resident rabbit to hop around a bit and play with her toys. It must also be tall enough for the rabbit to stand up on her hind legs to say hello to her family – and ideally without her ears butting up against the roof.

Your pet's cage must be big enough to divide into several areas. You may see rabbits in pet stores kept in smaller cages, but those crowded conditions are not what's best for your bunny.

SAFETY FIRST

When you look at cage features, safety is the number-one issue. Stainless steel wire is best; unlike wood, it cannot be gnawed and destroyed. The cage bars should be no more than two inches apart to prevent a trapped head or leg, and bar connections and corners should be smooth and free of sharp edges that could cut and injure the rabbit. And finally, for obvious reasons, make sure that the cage doors are secure and escape-proof. You don't want to find out the hard way that yours is one of those rabbits who is a consummate escape artist.

IS THE FLOOR COMFY?

While a wire cage floor is generally acceptable for a rabbit (and convenient for cleaning, especially if your rabbit doesn't use a litter box), your pet will probably be more comfortable with a solid cage floor that will offer her a greater sense of security. The solid floor will

also protect your pet's feet from injury or discomfort, and will most effectively support the various cage furnishings and bedding material within the rabbit's abode. Just make sure that the floor can be removed easily for cleaning.

Wooden hutches are traditional, but they do have drawbacks. Be prepared for chewing damage if you decide to house your bunny in a wooden hutch.

INTERIOR DECORATING

Clean little animal that she is, your rabbit will appreciate a living space designed in much the same way that your home is. When you're playing interior decorator for your pet, consider her natural instincts and habits and keep her "rooms" separated. Rabbits don't care to eat in the bathroom or sleep in the dining room. Your job, then, is to place the dining area (food dishes, hay rack, water bottle) in one corner of the cage, the litter box in another area, the nest box in an equally separate location, and toys in a play area – just as you would want your own home designed.

JUST THE RIGHT SPOT

Spend some time thinking about where to set up your rabbit's home. I have already discussed the fact that the home should be indoors with you for both health and bonding reasons. Beyond that, it should be situated someplace that will be safe and healthy for your rabbit. The ideal location is one that is protected from direct sunlight, heating or air-conditioning vents, and drafts, because excess heat or cold can be detrimental to a rabbit's health. Too much noise and activity can also be detrimental to this sensitive creature, who is, remember, a prey animal at heart. In the wild, your rabbit would spend a lot of time hiding. Place her cage in a quieter area of the house where she can rest easily and find solace from the stress of the busy parts of your house. Rabbits enjoy time spent out and about, but they also appreciate peace and quiet on the homefront.

Selective breeding has created some rabbits with ears that droop, called lop ears. These rabbits can't hear as well as rabbits with erect ears can.

A COZY BED

The final step in organizing your rabbit's home is the placement of the bedding and flooring. You may carpet the cage floor with newspaper, which is easy to remove for cleaning and gentle on the rabbit's feet. You should also provide your rabbit with bedding material on which she can rest more comfortably. This comfy material should carpet the floor of the nest box. Choose a bedding material that is designed specifically for rabbits, such as wood shavings (avoid cedar, which can be dangerous to a rabbit's respiratory system; aspen is generally considered safer), straw, or one of the recycled paper products. All of these are available at pet supply stores.

Hay   *Straw*

WELCOME HOME

It's an exciting day when a new pet comes home, but it's your job to make sure that excitement does not prove to be too stressful for the sensitive rabbit. Now is the time to restrain your exuberance and resist the urge to invite all your friends and neighbors over for a "welcome home bunny" party. First impressions are crucial to a rabbit, and you want to make sure that you and your pet start out on the right foot.

Bring your rabbit home in a secure travel carrier, preferably one that contains a bit of bedding material, a chew toy, and perhaps a treat or two. Greet the bunny quietly when you go to get her, allow her to sniff your hand and get acquainted with your scent, gently place her into the carrier, and keep the atmosphere as serene as you can on the drive home.

This peace and quiet should continue when you arrive home. Put the carrier down on the floor and lift your rabbit out gently. Place her into her new cage, which you have already prepared complete with full feeding dishes and water bottle. Don't worry, you'll have plenty of time for cuddling later when she gets used to her new home.

Don't demand too much from your pet at first. Keep voices soft and low, and handling gentle and to a minimum. Allow your new bunny time to get acquainted on her own terms. Resist the urge to sit and stare at the adorable critter who has just joined your family, and keep other family members from doing the same. The kids may protest, but there will be plenty of time later for admiring the bunny. Now you are setting the foundation of trust that will prove a valuable investment in your relationship for the days, months, and years to come.

This is not the time to introduce your new bunny to your dog or cat. As far as your rabbit is concerned, they are the predators and she is the prey! Give her time to settle in and feel safe before you make any introductions. Meanwhile, keep the door to the room your rabbit is in closed if you have other pets.

From this point on, take your cues from your rabbit as to how much social interaction she wishes to pursue with you and her new family. If you allow her time to adjust gradually to her new environment, your pet will probably start giving you signals that she's ready to get acquainted beyond the security of her cage – to be petted, lifted and held – sooner than she would if her homecoming is marked by stress and insecurity. Let your rabbit be your guide. She will appreciate your consideration and soon come to regard you as a fellow rabbit rather than as the human predator that, technically, you are.

PICKING UP A RABBIT

While it may seem obvious, it must be said anyway: Never, ever, ever lift a rabbit by her ears. Those lovely long ears may appear to be custom-made handles, but they are not. Picking up a rabbit by the ears can be grisly and painful for the victim of such an act, and it must be avoided at all costs. Speak to your children about this before the rabbit comes home, and don't just leave it to your kids to educate their friends. Make sure anyone who will be in contact with the rabbit knows the rules.

That said, we can move on to just how you should lift, carry, and hold a rabbit. First, remember that by nature rabbits don't really appreciate being lifted up into the air and held. While many can learn to tolerate it and actually enjoy it when the holder is a trusted caretaker, for many it stirs ancient memories of being lifted into the air by, say, an eagle intent on feeding this prey to her young. The key is to offer your rabbit a sense of security by providing her with full support as she's being lifted. An improperly supported rabbit can struggle, kick, fall, and sustain severe injuries. Here are two classic methods for secure rabbit handling.

A SMALL RABBIT

If yours is a small or very young rabbit, you may lift your pet in a manner similar to the way a mother rabbit carries her young. Take hold of the loose skin at the scruff of the rabbit's neck with one hand, slide the other hand beneath the bunny's rear end, and lift. Then, as soon as possible, nestle the rabbit's body against you, and support her underneath with one arm and hand. Hold your other hand over the animal's back for extra security.

A rabbit moves fast in leaps and bounds. Her powerful back legs kick out when she jumps. These kicks can hurt, and if you drop a kicking rabbit she can be injured. Protect your rabbit and yourself by picking her up carefully and securely.

A LARGE RABBIT

You can pick up a larger rabbit, or one whose natural response to handling is a kick, by sliding one hand beneath her chest between her two front legs, and the other beneath her rear end. Then lift the animal and bring her up against your body as quickly and as smoothly as possible. Tuck the bunny into the crook of your arm, offering support underneath her body with one arm (in the same position you would assume if you were carrying a football for a touchdown). Place your other hand over the rabbit's back to increase her sense of trust and security.

Regardless of the method you use, your goal is to prevent the rabbit from feeling as though she is dangling in mid-air or is in danger of falling. Achieving this goal may take some time and practice, especially if yours is a rabbit who has been handled improperly in the past. Be gentle and patient, and you may convince your pet that snuggling up next to you, even off the ground, isn't so bad after all.

WHAT BOX, WHERE?

Successful rabbit litter-box training revolves around the fact that, like most pet animals, rabbits do not like to relieve themselves in the same areas where they eat and sleep. Take advantage of this natural inclination and the rabbit's fastidious nature, and provide your pet with a special box located some distance from her dining and sleeping areas that she may use as a toilet. It may take time for the rabbit to understand this (and rabbits are rarely litter trained as "perfectly" as cats are), but with patience and praise you can convince your bunny to use the box some, if not most, of the time.

Rabbit litter boxes are identical to those used for cats. In fact, a smaller traditional cat box is ideal. You will actually need several litter boxes: one for the cage and the rest for the rooms of your house in which you allow your rabbit to run free. Yes, you'll need a box for each room – don't expect your bunny to go hopping off to another room to relieve herself. She'll be much more likely to use the box if it's nearby. As for the litter you use to fill the box, choose safe, natural, organic products composed of such materials as recycled paper, wheat, or similar litters designed especially for rabbits. Clay or wood-based products can prove too heavy for a rabbit, and may also cause respiratory problems.

While you will find an astonishing array of litter boxes at the store, rabbits prefer to keep things simple. Don't forget the scoop to remove waste.

Safe litters are light-weight and are made from natural materials.

Organic litter

Pressed litter pellets

KEEP IT CLEAN

Cleanliness is critical to litter box training success. Commit to cleaning up whenever your pet urinates or leaves a trail of fecal pellets in her wake, whether these are left in the box or out, in the cage or on the kitchen floor. Good hygiene benefits not only the overall health and well-being of your rabbit, but also your own sanity. It also keeps the odor associated with indoor rabbit keeping to a minimum.

Fecal pellets are easily picked up with a tissue, paper towel, or plastic bag wrapped around your hand. Urine may be cleaned up with soap and water from a hard floor. If it ends up on the carpet, use a mixture of water and white vinegar or one of the enzymatic, odor-eating products now available for pet clean-up. As for the box itself, remove fecal pellets and urine-soaked litter regularly (do the same with soiled areas of substrate on the cage floor; hence the benefit of a solid removable cage floor), and do a wholesale cleaning of the box once or twice a week. For this chore, remove all old litter, clean the box itself with water and mild soap or vinegar, rinse and dry well, and then fill the box with a fresh, clean litter.

LITTER BOX TRAINING

Once you have assembled the appropriate gear, the actual litter box training may begin. The first rule to remember for the effective and humane litter box training of a rabbit is that punishment has no place in the process. The secret ingredients are patience, consistency, and praise, no matter how long it takes for you to get the message across to your bunny. If you have a male rabbit, you might also enjoy greater success if you have your pet neutered, which will help prevent the territorial spraying behavior often common in intact male rabbits.

Begin your litter box training within the rabbit's cage. In other words, begin within a small confined area and broaden the horizons gradually as the rabbit shows that she understands what you are trying to teach her. Place a filled litter box within the cage, preferably in the corner your pet seems to have already chosen as her bathroom (pay attention when you're cleaning!). Place a few fecal pellets in the box to give your rabbit the right idea.

Your curious pet may hop right in to investigate. If she also happens to relieve herself, ample praise and a treat are in order. She may also simply sit in the box, and that's okay too. If she does this and also happens to munch on some hay, be encouraged that she has the right idea, since hay stimulates a rabbit gastrointestinally. Just be patient and ready with the praise. Place your rabbit in the box when you know she is likely to go (such as after meals). In time your bunny should get the message.

Once it seems the rabbit understands how she is supposed to use this new box, you can expand your efforts beyond the cage. Organize a confined area, perhaps the kitchen or a portion of a room that you cordon off with an extendible wire exercise pen like the type used for dogs, and place a new litter box there. Once again, be ready to praise your pet for demonstrating her good litter box habits.

In time, you can place several boxes in the corners of whatever room you have designated as a free-play zone for your rabbit (particularly in corners in which the rabbit has had "accidents" or has shown a special interest in occupying in the past). Keep an eye on your pet, don't expect one hundred percent compliance, and no matter how seasoned a veteran your pet is, be ever ready with the praise. A rabbit is never too old for a reminder of how wonderful she is and how proud you are of her performance.

RABBIT NUTRITION ESSENTIALS

A rabbit's basic nutritional requirements are not all that different from most species of mammals, including us. Rabbits require a variety of nutrients offered in a proper balance – usually in a combination of pellets, hay, and fresh greens – to keep their systems running smoothly. Nutrition, then, is an important step in helping house rabbits live the long, comfortable life span that is their birthright. The nutritional building blocks of the optimum rabbit diet include the following.

WATER
No living creature can survive without water, the most important nutritional component for rabbits and every mammal. Without water to facilitate cell function and overall system hydration, a rabbit can perish very quickly.

PROTEINS
Some of the most important structural tissues of the body – bone, muscle, blood – require a steady influx of high-quality protein for proper maintenance. Because rabbits are strict herbivores and derive all of their nutrients from plant sources, they must get their proteins from plant sources. Only a variety of food will enable them to get all the proteins they need.

FATS AND CARBOHYDRATES

A rabbit's energy needs are fueled by the presence of fats and carbohydrates in her diet, but as with all nutrients the rabbit ingests each day, these must be properly balanced within the bunny's daily food ration. An overabundance of carbohydrates and fats (the latter of which are higher in energy than the former) can lead to what is considered the number-one health problems in pet rabbits today: obesity. Excess energy nutrients are stored in the rabbit's body and result not only in excess weight, but also in a potentially shortened and uncomfortable life span.

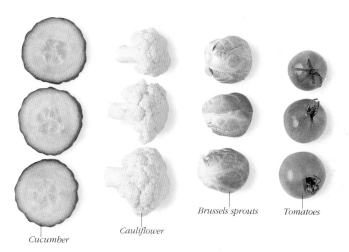

Brussels sprouts *Tomatoes*

Cauliflower

Cucumber

VITAMINS AND MINERALS

It's no secret that vitamins and minerals play important roles in just about every bodily function in an animal's body. What many people don't understand, however, is that vitamins and minerals must be balanced or those functions can severely misfire. Family pets are frequently the victims of well-intentioned caretakers who overdose their charges with vitamin and mineral supplements. Fortunately, much is known today about a rabbit's nutritional needs, and foods are readily available to satisfy those needs simply and effectively through the animals' basic diet. Vitamin and mineral supplementation is rarely required if the rabbit is receiving a well-balanced basic rabbit diet.

A RABBIT'S DIET

Pellets, hay, and fresh greens and fruit – these are the components of the healthy rabbit's basic diet. Feeding your classic vegetarian is rather inexpensive. It can also be fun. The following guidelines will help you collect the right foods for a balanced rabbit diet.

Hay___

___Rabbit pellets

PELLETS
Available at most pet supply stores, high-quality rabbit pellets will offer your pet an excellent balance of nutrients. Make sure the pellets you buy are fresh, and resist the impulse to stock up on a year's supply at a time, because pellets can spoil (a month's supply or so is a safer bet). There was a time when rabbit keepers thought pellets were all a rabbit required for health and vitality, but we now know this is not true.

HAY
A rabbit's system thrives best when supplemented with a regular ration of hay – preferably timothy hay, and preferably hay that is sold specifically for rabbits at pet supply stores. Fill your rabbit's hay rack only with hay that is fresh, clean and sweet-smelling. Spoiled hay can have terrible effects on your pet's system.

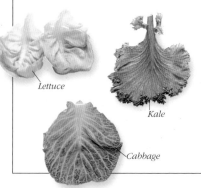

Lettuce

Kale

Cabbage

FRESH GREENS
Although rabbits are frequently depicted munching on carrots, dark, fresh greens such as spinach, dandelion greens, carrot tops, and romaine lettuce are better choices for your pet. These are healthy additions to your rabbit's diet, and will also keep mealtimes more interesting.

Fresh Fruit
Pieces of apple, pear, or melon all make good snacks for your rabbit. Just a little will go a long way with these tasty snacks.

Treats
Because of the pet rabbit's predisposition to obesity, treats should be kept to a minimum – and then only in the healthiest, most natural form. Treat your pet with pieces of fruit; dried, pesticide-free branches from fruit trees; and commercial treats formulated specifically for rabbits.

Supplements
Because the core of the rabbit's diet provides the animal with the proper balance of nutrients she requires, it's usually best to steer clear of nutritional supplements that could potentially throw your pet's finely balanced diet out of balance. So skip the supplements unless directed to do so by your pet's veterinarian.

Cecotropes
As a rabbit owner, you must accept the fact that there will be times when your rabbit will excrete small pellets from her anus and then eat them. These are not feces. These soft pellets, called cecotropes, are produced within the rabbit's intestines and are one supplement your rabbit does require for overall health. As disconcerting as the concept may be, allow your pet to act on her impulse. Your bunny knows best.

Because a rabbit's stomach can't extract all the nutrients from her food, cecotropes are her way of getting the goodness she missed out on the first time. They are softer than fecal pellets.

A FEEDING SCHEDULE

While it's a rare human who gets fat from eating too many vegetables, pet rabbits do tend to be overweight because they eat more and exercise less than their wild cousins. And a fat rabbit is not as healthy, and thus not as contented, as she should be. Once you understand that you must resist the urge to overfeed, feeding a rabbit properly is far from complicated. And by committing to a healthy diet and the right feeding regimen, you can help maintain your pet's optimum condition for years to come.

Offer your rabbit pellets, hay and fresh fruits and vegetables in separate dishes, so she can choose what to nibble on. And throw away all uneaten food, including hay, at the end of the day.

A feeding regimen is determined by the rabbit's size and, to a lesser extent, by her age. A young rabbit may be given constant access to a dish of pellets to fuel her growth, but once she reaches it first birthday or so, your pet's pellet consumption should become more controlled. A small rabbit, say a two- to four-pound dwarf variety, will require approximately one ounce of pellets a day, divided into two feedings (morning and evening, just as rabbits schedule mealtimes in the wild). A larger rabbit – one weighing between ten and fifteen pounds – will require about six ounces in two feedings, while the bunny in the middle will thrive best on a four-ounce daily pellet ration. Offer pellets in a clean, sturdy ceramic or hard plastic dish with a weighted bottom to prevent tipping.

As for hay, fill the hay rack each day with a handful of fresh, clean hay and throw away any old hay to avoid spoilage (do the same with old pellets between feedings).

Fresh greens should also be offered each day. Provide two or three different varieties in a separate heavy-bottomed rabbit dish. And again, throw away leftovers between feedings.

FRESH WATER DAILY

And last, but certainly not least, don't forget the water. Your pet should have access to fresh, clean water twenty-four hours a day. Water is most effectively served in a water bottle with a sipping tube that is anchored to the side of the cage. You may even want to install two bottles in case one tube becomes clogged, especially if you will be leaving your rabbit alone for a weekend while you are traveling.

Refill the water bottle with fresh water every day, and check to make sure the tube is not clogged or leaking.

BORN TO CHEW

Rabbits need to chew. They are compelled to chew, they are driven to chew, and if they are unable to chew they can suffer unbearable dental pain, infection, and mouth punctures, not to mention severe malnutrition because of their inability to eat.

Check your rabbit's front teeth regularly by carefully pushing back her lips. The teeth should be clean and straight. If they appear to be crooked or too long, visit your veterinarian.

Wild rabbits eat hard food, which wears down their teeth. But a domestic rabbit's diet won't do the job. Your bunny needs hard things to chew.

A rabbit's incisors, like those of a rodent, are constantly growing. The chewing action is designed to keep the rabbit's teeth trimmed, sharp, honed, and healthy – and the rabbit properly nourished. A rabbit cursed with an improperly aligned jaw, resulting in overgrown teeth and their attendant problems, must regularly have her teeth trimmed by the veterinarian or she will not thrive.

PICK SAFE CHEW TOYS

Since your rabbit must chew, you are responsible for providing your pet with things to chew that are safe and beneficial. If you don't, your rabbit will seek out her own chewing items, and these probably won't be things you wanted chewed up by a rabbit. Rabbits aren't choosy about their chew toys, and they will willingly munch upon your new Berber carpet or the antique armoire you inherited from your great-grandmother. These kinds of casualties are common among rabbit owners.

You can find rabbit chew toys and specially treated wood blocks in pet supply stores. Your rabbit will also enjoy dried, aged branches and twigs from fruit trees, as long as you are certain the trees have never been sprayed with pesticides. You might even try rotating the chew toys (as parents often do with their toddlers' toys), to keep things new and interesting.

Offer ample choices to your rabbit both inside and outside of her cage, and keep a close eye on your pet when she's at liberty hopping about your home. If you don't, she'll turn your house into one big chew toy.

RABBIT AEROBICS

Although rabbits may seem quiet and unassuming, like all pets they require exercise to keep them – and their owners – sane. A rabbit who does not get enough exercise and social inter-action with her family can become neurotic and develop bad habits, such as chewing on the wire of her cage or thumping incessantly because of all that pent-up energy. She will eventually go crazy from boredom and inactivity.

Again, we look to wild rabbits for clues to what our pet rabbits require. While their territory may not typically be extensive, wild rabbits spend a great deal of their time traversing that territory searching for food, and in the process stretching those long legs of theirs and stimulating their rather intelligent minds. These are very active creatures, known for their speed, smarts, and endurance.

Owners of domestic rabbits are wise to offer their pets similar opportunities to pursue and satisfy their natural need for activity. But that doesn't mean putting your rabbit in a bigger space in the house or backyard on her own. Remember, wild rabbits live in social groups, and your pet has a natural desire for social interactions with her family. So the best way to give her exercise is as part of activities she does with you. This requires some effort on your part, but remember, this is a very intelligent, sensitive, social creature who needs you to play an active role in her life. And if you don't want to interact with your rabbit every day, why do you want a rabbit?

A variety of activities will also keep a rabbit stimulated and entertained. The animal would frankly rather not do exactly the same thing every day (would you?), or even chew on the same toys. Be creative, remain committed to your pet's need for exercise, and try to make sure that the bunny has access to some sort of activity each and every day.

MORE THAN ONE?

Rabbits do enjoy living with other rabbits, but territorial disputes can arise when they are housed together. Each rabbit should therefore be provided with her own cage. They will probably play together, but you must supervise all interactions, just in case. And, given the rabbit's phenomenal reproduction rates, make sure you have your pets spayed or neutered. This will cut down on any territorial disputes, and keep your home from being overrun by bunnies.

An outdoor playpen is an ideal place to play with your rabbit when the weather is nice.

RABBIT-PROOFING YOUR HOUSE

A pet rabbit cannot spend her entire life in a cage. This smart, active animal requires time spent out and about, no matter how spacious and well-appointed that cage may be. You need to supervise your rabbit when she's out of her cage, so plan to make time for her every day. It's your job to spend time with the rabbit and keep tabs on her movements and activities, and it's also your responsibility to rabbit-proof the premises to keep your pet safe and alive while she enjoys her time at liberty.

Rabbits can get themselves into plenty of trouble – and danger. Before you even think of allowing your rabbit to explore beyond her cage door, you must investigate the area from a rabbit's-eye view. Get on the floor and start sniffing around. You'll no doubt find items that will instantly attract the attention – and chewing activity – of a curious rabbit. Topping this list will be electrical cords (which can cause injury, death, and fire), carpeting, wood furniture, books, shoes, houseplants, and anything else a rabbit can get her teeth on.

Before you allow your rabbit out and about, lift up electrical cords out of the rabbit's reach (unplug them if you must), remove chewable items from the floor, put the houseplants up high, and block the bunny's access to favored corners where the carpeting is easiest to chew. Make sure there's nothing she could get stuck under or in.

While your bunny is out, keep a close eye on her so you can gently remove and distract her from inappropriate and unsafe behavior. You may also be able to divert her from gnawing on wood furniture by applying a safe pet repellent to wood surfaces. These products, such as Bitter Apple, give a bad taste to whatever you spray them on. And finally, don't forget to set out those litter boxes, which can make your pet's time outside of her cage more pleasant for everyone.

RABBIT-PROOFING YOUR YARD

Just as you must rabbit-proof your home to accommodate your pet, do the same outdoors. Again, let your pet's safety be your guide. Ideally, choose an area that is confined (such as a fenced backyard), and make sure there will be no surprise visits from dogs, cats, or other predators. Examine the fencing and remember that rabbits are natural burrowers. If given the chance, they can dig their way under flimsy fencing and escape before you have even realized what has happened.

Since it's inevitable that your vegetarian will sample the local greenery, make sure all the plants she has access to are safe for her to chew. There should be no poisonous plants, cactus, or thornbushes in the area where your bunny will be playing. You must also be sure all the plants she has access to are free from pesticides and fertilizers.

Once you deem the premises safe, you may feel confident allowing your pet to explore the yard at liberty – especially if the yard contains a garden through which you allow your rabbit to rummage. It's typically safer, however, to build your own confined outdoor play area for your rabbit using an exercise pen or large wire crate made for dogs. Anchored securely, these can permit your pet to hop around in complete safety in the sunshine, nibbling on the grass and dandelions to her heart's delight.

Make sure that your pet has access to water, shelter, and shade while she's in her outdoor playpen, because direct sunlight and inclement weather can be detrimental to your rabbit's health and comfort. And never put your rabbit outside when it's too hot or too chilly for you to be comfortably outside.

Whenever you are outdoors with your rabbit, keep your eyes open. You can't just send your rabbit outdoors to fend for herself while you go about your business indoors. You could end up with an injured rabbit – or no rabbit at all. Watching your pet play and explore in the great outdoors is an experience that you'll probably enjoy as much as your rabbit does.

TAKE YOUR BUNNY FOR A WALK

It's a startling sight to see a rabbit out and about on a leash with her owner, yet it's becoming more commonplace every day. Not every rabbit can be leash trained, but it's certainly worth a try. You'll need lots of patience, and a sense of humor.

You will first need to buy a special harness and leash appropriate for a rabbit. These are available from most pet supply stores, and are marketed specifically for rabbits. They are usually made of nylon cord and sometimes already have a leash attached. Make sure you buy a harness that will not tighten if your rabbit gets a little bit ahead of you while you are walking. Place the harness on your rabbit – not too tight, not too loose – and let her wear the contraption for brief periods of time as she hops about the house. Once the rabbit is accustomed to the harness (which could take days, weeks, or never happen), attach the leash and let your pet drag it around for a while. Then hold on to the leash and see how the bunny responds to that. You may want to offer treats occasionally as bribes to inspire her cooperation. Just be patient, and you may be rewarded in the end with a rabbit who enjoys hopping along at the end of a leash. Or you may not be, and that's okay, too. Then your bunny can enjoy the great outdoors in her backyard playpen.

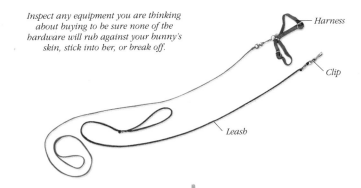

Inspect any equipment you are thinking about buying to be sure none of the hardware will rub against your bunny's skin, stick into her, or break off.

Harness

Clip

Leash

THE RABBIT WALKS YOU

If your rabbit is one of the amenable ones, you can eventually take her outside on her leash. Begin in a quiet, safe area, such as your fenced backyard. If you succeed you may expand to more public areas – a park or your neighborhood sidewalk.

Just remember that you are walking a rabbit, not a dog. Pulling on the leash or forcing the rabbit to follow you or to heel like a dog is not allowed. In a sense, the rabbit will be walking you. The bunny will hop along and you will follow – but you must remain alert. You can't allow your pet to worm her way into dangerous situations involving poisonous plants, open manhole covers, busy streets, unruly kids, dogs, cats, broken glass, garbage, automobiles, and so on. Be prepared to jump in and whisk your pet out of harm's way at even the slightest hint of danger, and hold your pet safely and securely until the danger has passed.

RABBIT PLAYTIME

The sky's the limit when it comes to the fun you can have with your rabbit, once everything has been made safe and ready for your pet. While you may be inspired by the idea of allowing your pet free run of your entire home, it's simpler, and safer, to designate certain rooms – say, the kitchen and the family room – as bunny-friendly zones, and manage your pet's activities in these rooms accordingly.

The activities you choose for your rabbit's time spent out of her cage can run the gamut from games with rabbit toys to just sitting on the couch watching television with your rabbit on your lap. Whatever you do, you'll both enjoy the interaction.

HIDE THE FOOD
One of the ways you can play with your rabbit out of her cage is to hide some of her food and let her find it. This is just what she'd do in the wild. Try turning a clean flowerpot on its side and putting a piece of fruit in it, or put a yummy leaf of kale under a towel with just a bit sticking out so your bunny can find it.

Rabbits have a very keen sense of smell, and will investigate new things by smelling them. When you take your rabbit out of her cage, you are exposing her to a world of interesting smells that, for her, are much like reading a newspaper.

YOUR RABBIT NEEDS TOYS

Toys can offer your pet unlimited entertainment, especially if you rotate a variety of toys each day or reserve certain toys only for play outside the cage. Toys can range from small, lightweight balls that a rabbit can chase or bat, cardboard paper towel roll that your pet may enjoy pushing and rolling on the floor or simply chewing, or novelty rabbit toys that are available at pet supply stores.

Some rabbits have even been known to enjoy a rousing game of chase-the-cat, but that is hardly the norm. And insisting that your rabbit play with any other animal can result in severe rabbit stress, distrust, injury, and even illness. Let your bunny take the lead in any cross-species interactions.

Listen to your pet. Each rabbit has her own specific likes and dislikes. Your pet will make her preferences known without hesitation. Get involved with your rabbit, and, whether or not you are invited to join in the game, you'll be amazed at how pleasurable it can be just to watch this adorable, intelligent little animal explore and interact with her world.

Accept the fact that your bunny is going to chew on just about everything you give her. That's what rabbits do!

41

A RABBIT DICTIONARY

Rabbits are some of the quietest of pets. That's because in the wild prey animals are better off remaining as unobtrusive as possible. But while rabbits aren't very loud, they have developed a very complex vocabulary comprised of both vocalizations and body language. If you pay attention to your pet, you will come to understand what she is trying to tell you and enjoy an even more satisfying bond. These guidelines on the basics of rabbit language, combined with the time you spend personally with your pet, should give you a head start at mastering rabbit speak.

CONTENTMENT

When she's happy and relaxed, your rabbit may purr like a cat, make a clicking sound, or grind her teeth softly (loud grinding indicates pain). The contented bunny will squat down in a relaxed position, conveying with her posture and her expression that all is right with the world. Rabbits do kick out if they're uncomfortable or nervous, but they also kick with pleasure during play, so pay attention to the context of the situation. If your pet is feeling particularly confident, she may hop about rubbing her chin on certain household items and landmarks, broadcasting the fact that this territory belongs to this rabbit. As for staking a claim on her caretaker, the rabbit may lick your skin in a complimentary show of mutual grooming behavior.

DISPLEASURE

It's not all that difficult to tell when your rabbit is discontented or nervous. It's most graphically apparent when she shakes her ears or kicks out vigorously in response to, say, someone who is carrying her improperly. (These vigorous kicks can lead to back and leg injuries, so try not to provoke them in your rabbit.) If you hear your rabbit hiss, perhaps at something that frightened her, take that as a definite sign of displeasure or aggression. Regard the hiss, as well as the other physical messages, as a hint that some changes to the current situation are in order.

FEAR

Hear a rabbit scream and you won't doubt for a minute the message: Your pet is in fear for her life. The same is true when the rabbit flattens her body to the ground (in an effort to make herself invisible to predators), or thumps her foot, a signal of warning in response to a perceived threat – whether genuine or imagined (those prey instincts, remember). Take your rabbit's fear seriously, even when you know there's no real threat. View every situation through your pet's eyes and you can prevent the circumstances that might inspire her to respond with fear.

A fearful rabbit might press herself close to the ground. In the wild, this would help her hide herself in the grass or underbrush.

INTRODUCING KIDS AND OTHER PETS

One situation that can lead to rabbit fear and stress is the presence of children or other pets, most of which qualify as predators to your little prey animal. Yet many a rabbit has come to enjoy the attentions of an extended family of humans of all ages and animals of various species (some rabbits even come to dominate the family cat or dog). The secret is a gradual introduction and constant supervision. Before introducing young children and other pets to the new rabbit, let the newcomer get acquainted with her cage, with you, and with the scents within her new home for a few days, and you'll increase your chances of success.

Keep hold of the dog's leash so you are sure you can control him if he decides a rabbit looks a lot like a prey animal.

RABBITS AND KIDS

You may invite the kids in to take a look at the rabbit, but instruct them to keep their voices soft and quiet in the presence of the rabbit and her very sensitive ears (now and always). As your bunny grows more comfortable, allow the children to pet her while she's in your lap. Very gradually increase the duration and nature of their interaction, all the while monitoring the situation to make sure all encounters remain civilized and stress free.

In time, a genuine trust and camaraderie can develop between kids and their pet rabbit. Just remember that children should never be left unattended with the rabbit, nor should they be allowed to handle her in a rough manner or view her as a toy.

RABBITS AND OTHER PETS

While rabbits tend to get along well with others of their own kind (evident in their staggering reproduction rates), cats and dogs represent predators. The rules of engagement here are not all that different from those that govern your rabbit's interaction with children.

Sit down, hold the rabbit securely on your lap, and allow the bunny first to just observe her new prospective friend. When the rabbit is ready (which may take days), allow the dog or cat to come forward so they may sniff one another. Gradually increase the duration of the time they spend together until you decide it's safe to place the rabbit on the floor. Be ready to whisk the rabbit up and away should things go awry, and provide your rabbit with a safe place to which she may run and hide if she is frightened. You may be rewarded with two animals (or more) that develop a genuine respect and affection for one another. Or not. Accept that possibility and you'll all live happier ever after.

FORGET NOAH'S ARK
Some cats and dogs are just too predatory to ever form a friendship with a lagomorph. Watch carefully the first few times you introduce them, and be honest in your evaluations. You may have to accept the fact that your various pets will never be friends. And that's just fine. As for the dog or cat that is a viable candidate, commit from the beginning to supervise all interactions – always.

RABBITS LIKE THINGS CLEAN

Most animals are inherently clean. They know instinctively that they must be, because allowing their skin and hair to become filthy, or living in a home infested with dirt and parasites invites weakness, illness, and premature death. The rabbit is no exception, and will only thrive with caretakers who are equally dedicated to a regimen of fastidious cleanliness, both for the rabbit herself and for her habitat.

THE CAGE CLEANING CHECKLIST

You must keep a bunny's habitat clean and pristine, and that means daily, weekly, and monthly chores. The rabbit does her part to help simplify the process simply by the way she lives. But you must do your part as well. A rabbit thrives best, both in the wild and in your home, when her living space is divided into distinct sleeping, eating, playing, and bathroom areas. Each mess the rabbit makes is thus localized, so you don't have to pick up a mish-mash of residual food, soaked newspaper, hay, and fecal pellets every day. But you do have to pick up.

DAILY

- ○ Remove all uneaten food from the cage floor at the end of each day.
- ○ Remove uneaten pellets from the food dish between the morning and evening feedings.
- ○ Remove any uneaten fruit or vegetables at the end of the day.
- ○ Remove any uneaten hay and replace it with fresh hay.
- ○ Change the water in the water bottle and inspect the drinking tube for blockages.

○ Remove newspaper layers on the floor that are soiled by food or urine.
○ Remove fecal pellets from the cage floor and the litter box.
○ Remove wet and otherwise soiled litter from the litter box.

WEEKLY OR TWICE A WEEK

○ Scrub the water bottle and feeding dishes with water and white vinegar or mild soap. Rinse well and dry before placing them back in the cage.
○ Dispose of old litter in the litter box, scrub the litter box with a vinegar or soap and water mixture, and fill the box with a clean, fresh supply of litter.
○ Remove newspaper flooring, scrub the cage floor with a soap or vinegar and water mixture, and cover it with several layers of fresh newspaper (several layers will make daily removal easier).
○ Remove old bedding from the nest box and replace with a fresh new supply.

MONTHLY

○ Scrub the cage structure itself – walls and floor – with water and white vinegar or mild soap. Rinse and dry well before replacing the cage furnishings and the resident rabbit.
○ Scrub the nest box, your bunny's toys, and everything else your bunny uses.

EVEN GREAT GROOMERS NEED HELP

Once you have spent some time with your new pet rabbit, you may begin to believe that she has been possessed by a cat spirit. Rabbits give cats a definite run for their money when it comes to the title of most meticulous groomer. Both spend a great deal of time each day grooming themselves, and in doing so, contort their bodies into unbelievable positions to ensure they clean every nook and cranny. It's fun to watch a rabbit do these grooming acrobatics, licking her fur with her tongue, washing her face with her paws, tending to herself quite lovingly.

Still, your bunny needs some help from you. While most of your dedication to rabbit cleanliness will translate into time spent cleaning her cage, your rabbit also needs help with her grooming.

One drawback of that meticulous attention to grooming detail is that, like a cat, the fastidious self-grooming rabbit can end up swallowing a great deal of her thick, lovely fur. This can lead to a buildup of hair within the gastrointestinal tract which, if severe, will require veterinary intervention. The more you brush out regularly, the less your bunny will swallow. It's that simple.

Besides helping to remove loose hair, brushing and combing stimulates the distribution of skin oils, and offers you the opportunity to look for signs – lumps, bumps, fleas and such – that require veterinary attention. This quick once-over will tell you what is normal and what is abnormal so that should a problem arise, you will catch it early and be able to tell the veterinarian about it. For example, if you find a lump under the skin on the rabbit's ribcage, you will be able to tell your vet that you brushed your rabbit on Friday evening and the lump wasn't there, but when you combed her on Sunday it was. You can also let him know whether it is painful for your rabbit, feels hot, moves under your fingers, or any other details that could help your veterinarian diagnose and treat your rabbit.

While you're at it, examine the ears, too, to check for a waxy buildup or unusual odors. Hold the ear very gently between your fingers and look down the canal. Pick up each paw and check that the pads and the spaces between the toes are clean. This exercise will also tell you when your rabbit's nails need to be trimmed. Look in your pet's eyes, too. The eyelids should be wide open and the eyes should be clear and shiny.

If you neglect your grooming duties, you will not only end up with a discontented, possibly ill, even neurotic bunny on your hands, but also an odor within your home that should not be associated with the keeping of such a naturally clean pet as the domestic rabbit.

A GROOMING ROUTINE

One way to spend quality time with your pet rabbit is through regular grooming sessions. While your rabbit will spend a great deal of time grooming herself, she will be happier and healthier if you participate in this task as well. Your duties will involve brushing, combing, and nail trimming. Given the soft, lustrous texture of a rabbit's coat, grooming can be a pleasurable experience for you both.

Metal-tooth comb

Bristle brush

THE RABBIT HAIRDRESSER

Use a soft bristle brush and a metal comb to groom your rabbit. Try to brush and comb your bunny at least once a week. If she is a longhaired variety, you'll have to brush her every day or every other day.

To brush a shorthaired rabbit, brush the hair back away from her head and toward her rump, with the natural lie of the hair. Next, brush the belly and under her chin. Then comb all the parts in the same order.

To brush a longhaired variety such as a cashmere or angora bunny, groom the coat a little bit at a time. Brush and then comb a small part, then move on to the next part.

THE RABBIT MANICURE

When you notice that the nails are getting long, wrap your pet in a towel, place her on your lap and clip off the tips of the nails with a traditional toenail clipper. You'll see a pink part extending down the nail, but ending before the tip. This is the quick, and you don't want to cut it. Cut just the tip of the nail that extends beyond the quick.

This may be easier said than done. If you cut too deeply into the quick the nail will bleed, so it's wise to keep a tin of blood-stopping powder handy just in case. You may find that your rabbit absolutely refuses to cooperate with the procedure, in which case you may want to reserve this task for the veterinarian. You might also try to work to convince your pet, with treats and one or two nails per session, that it's really not as bad as it seems. Either way, the nails must be trimmed, and, like all grooming tasks, it must be done regularly.

An angora rabbit will need to be brushed and combed every day.

WORKING WITH A VETERINARIAN

You are the first line of defense in the care and maintenance of your pet rabbit's health and well-being. Interacting with your pet every day, you become intimately familiar with what is normal for her, and you are thus prepared to note immediately when something changes, either physically or behaviorally. Routine grooming sessions will acquaint you with your pet's health, as will regular evaluations of what you find in the litter box (diarrhea or hairballs, perhaps), and your observations of your rabbit's play, toilet, and eating behaviors.

Because rabbits are becoming more popular as pets, veterinarians are learning more about what we need to do to keep them healthy.

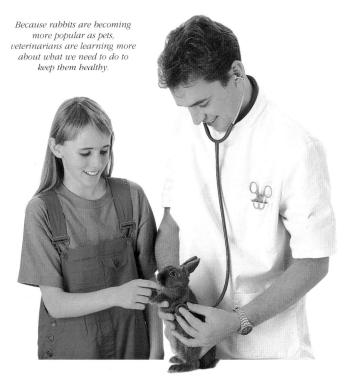

Your partner in this mission is your rabbit's veterinarian, whom you should not hesitate to call if you suspect even a minor problem. Your rabbit's veterinarian will appreciate an owner who is attuned to his or her pet's health and is prepared to seek veterinary attention in the earliest stages of a potential health problem.

Your first visit to the veterinarian should be for an overall examination of your new pet. This will help the veterinarian establish what is normal for your rabbit.

Not every veterinarian is qualified to care for rabbits, although today many more veterinarians are gaining this expertise. Check out the practitioners in your area as soon as you start thinking about getting a rabbit, and you'll be ready once your pet is in need of veterinary care.

SPAY OR NEUTER YOUR RABBIT
At your bunny's first visit, it's wise to schedule an appointment to have your rabbit spayed or neutered. Fortunately for rabbits, these procedures have become commonplace among pet bunnies, and a boon to their health and contentment as pets. Spayed and neutered rabbits make better, more relaxed pets. This is especially evident in neutered males, who are far less aggressive, territorial, and prone to spraying behavior than intact males. They also make healthier pets, because altering helps to prevent various cancers that can prematurely claim the lives of pet rabbits.

SIGNS OF HEALTH AND ILLNESS

Pet rabbits can live for up to ten years or more in a clean, pristine environment with proper nutrition and under the care of nurturing, diligent owners. There is no mistaking the vision that is a healthy rabbit. But as the guardian of your pet rabbit's health, you must remain ever vigilant to the various signs that could mean your bunny is ailing.

THE HEALTHY RABBIT
- ○ Bright, intelligent eyes
- ○ An alert expression enhanced by an ever-wriggling nose
- ○ Clean ears untainted by odor or a waxy buildup
- ○ A solid, properly proportioned physique
- ○ Clean, balanced movement
- ○ A soft, clean, evenly textured coat of fur
- ○ Clean, moist skin
- ○ An overall curious nature

Weight your pet regularly. If your rabbit has lost weight, she may be ill. If she's gained weight, she may not be getting enough exercise.

WHEN TO CALL YOUR BUNNY'S VETERINARIAN

- Loss of appetite or difficulty eating
- Diarrhea or constipation
- Hair or worms in the litter box
- Lethargy and listlessness
- Dull eyes
- Discharge from the nose or eyes
- Dull, dry fur
- Scaly, dry skin
- Lumps or bumps on the skin
- Fleas and/or flea dirt (flea excrement), which looks like dark red flecks
- Weight loss
- Obesity
- Odor and/or wax in the ears
- Breathing difficulties, wheezing
- Loud teeth grinding
- Bloated abdomen
- Obvious pain or injury

SERIOUS HEALTH PROBLEMS

Rabbits tend to be rather healthy as a species, but they can fall prey to health problems and diseases. All of these problems listed here require veterinary attention.

PARASITES

Parasites can afflict a rabbit both inside and out. Topping the list of the external bugs are fleas, which can cause intense discomfort to a rabbit and must be treated only under the guidance of a veterinarian to prevent a toxic reaction.

Internally, worms are a danger, including tapeworms (transmitted by fleas) and roundworms (usually picked up from dog feces). A bloated abdomen, a dull coat and the presence of worms in the litter box are evidence of a worm infestation, which must be treated by a veterinarian.

DISEASE

Two common diseases that affect the pet rabbit population are coccidiosis, a protozoal disease of the gastrointestinal tract, and myxomatosis, an essentially fatal viral illness that was deliberately introduced to eradicate wild rabbit populations in Europe in the nineteenth century. Both are more easily prevented than treated by keeping pet rabbits indoors in cages that are clean and properly maintained.

EMERGENCY FIRST AID

Emergencies are rare in the lives of pet rabbits, but they can occur. Most involve broken bones or bleeding wounds sustained around the home. Most rabbit owners are not qualified to care for or diagnose such conditions, and the mishandling of so small an animal can only lead to greater injury. Your mission, then, is to restrain the animal to prevent further injury, control bleeding, and get the rabbit to the veterinarian as soon as possible (even if a wound looks small, it could be a deep puncture wound). A towel wrapped around the animal's body to immobilize the patient can accomplish the first goal. As for the second, apply direct pressure to a wound with a clean gauze pad or a towel to stop bleeding, and keep the patient as still as possible. Place the rabbit in a travel carrier for the journey to the animal hospital.

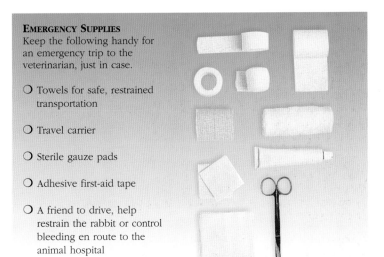

EMERGENCY SUPPLIES
Keep the following handy for an emergency trip to the veterinarian, just in case.

○ Towels for safe, restrained transportation

○ Travel carrier

○ Sterile gauze pads

○ Adhesive first-aid tape

○ A friend to drive, help restrain the rabbit or control bleeding en route to the animal hospital

YOUR RABBIT NEEDS YOU

The pet rabbit is far more than a creature with a whisper-soft coat of fur, long ears, and an ever-twitching nose. The rabbit is, in fact, the product of a rich heritage that has combined both the species' natural wild instincts and character, and the careful intervention of humans – all resulting in one of our most popular pets today. So invite a rabbit into your home, and honor your pet by offering her the care and nurturing she requires.

While the recipe for maintaining the health and well-being of a pet rabbit includes everything from nutrition to veterinary care to routine cage cleaning, the most important ingredient, the one that overrides and guides all others, is love. Love is the foundation of the bond that leads us to live with animals in the first place, and when lavished upon the very sociable creature that is the domestic rabbit, our effort is returned tenfold and more.

When you invite a rabbit in to share your home, you enter into a mutual contract. The bunny enters the arrangement ready and willing to satisfy your primal longing to live with a creature of wild ancestry who possesses a magical ability to touch the human soul with her quiet brand of unconditional acceptance and affection. You, in turn, must provide this animal with all she requires not only to lead a healthy domestic existence, but also to thrive emotionally in a life as fulfilling as what she would experience if she were a member of an extended rabbit colony in the wild.

Your rabbit depends on you to play surrogate rabbit and to take seriously the great responsibilities that honor entails. Your pet has faith that you will live up to that calling, knowing you'll both be profoundly enriched for the experience.

MORE TO LEARN

RABBIT ASSOCIATIONS

The American Rabbit Breeders
Association
PO Box 426
Bloomington, IL 61702
(309) 664-7500
members.aol.com/arbanet/
arba/web/

The House Rabbit Rescue Network
PO Box 33364
Austin, TX 78764-3364
(512) 444-EARS

The House Rabbit Society
1524 Benton Street
Alameda, CA 94501
www.rabbit.org

BOOKS

Dwarf Rabbits: A Complete Pet Owner's Manual, by Monika Wegler and Elizabeth D. Crawford (translator), Barron's Educational Series

Hop to It: A Guide to Training Your Pet Rabbit, by Samantha Hunter and Samantha Fraser, Barron's Educational Series

House Rabbit Handbook: How to Live With an Urban Rabbit, by Marinell Harriman, Drollery Press

Proper Care of Rabbits, by Darlene Campbell, TFH Publications

The Rabbit: An Owner's Guide to a Happy Healthy Pet, by Audrey Pavia, Howell Book House

Why Does My Rabbit...? by Anne McBride, Souvenir Press Ltd.

WEB SITES

The Bunny Thymes Home Page
www.cyberus.ca/~buntales

The Hoppin' Rabbit Page
www.angelfire.com/nc/rabbit

Mailing Lists and Newsgroups
www.rabbit.org/links/sections/
mailing-lists.html

The Rabbit Education Society
www.geocities/Heartland/Valley/
1155/RES.html

Rabbits Online
www.jarvis98.freeserve.co.uk

MAGAZINES

Rabbits Annual
Fancy Publications Inc.
P.O. Box 6050
Mission Viejo, CA 92690
(714) 855-8822

Rabbits Only
P.O. Box 207
Holbrook, NY 11741
(516) 737-0763

ABOUT THE AUTHOR

Betsy Sikora Siino is an award-winning author who has written almost 20 books and hundreds of articles on animals – all kinds of animals – and their care. Some of her most recent books include *For the Life of Your Dog* (with Olympic gold medalist Greg Louganis) and *The Complete Idiot's Guide to Choosing a Pet*. In addition to her concern for the care and well-being of companion animals, Betsy has a special interest in children and animals, the human-animal bond, and the preservation and survival of wild species.

INDEX

Dorling DK Kindersley

LONDON, NEW YORK, SYDNEY, DELHI, PARIS,
MUNICH, JOHANNESBURG

Project Editor: Beth Adelman
Design: Carol Wells, Annemarie Redmond
Cover Design: Gus Yoo
Photo Research: Mark Dennis
Index: Nanette Cardon

Photo Credits: Steve Gorton, Dave King, Tim Ridley, Tim Shepard, Steve Shott

First American Edition, 2000
2 4 6 8 10 9 7 5 3 1

Published in the United States by
Dorling Kindersley Publishing, Inc. 95 Madison Avenue New York, New York 10016

Dorling Kindersley Publishing, Inc. offers special discounts for bulk purchases for sales promotion
or premiums. Specific, large-quantity needs can be met with special editions, including
personalized covers, excerpts of existing guides, and corporate imprints. For more information,
contact Special Markets Department, Dorling Kindersley Publishing, Inc.,
95 Madison Avenue, New York, NY 10016 Fax: (800) 600-9098.

Color reproduction by Colourscan, Singapore
Printed in Hong Kong by Wing King Tong

Library of Congress Cataloging-in-Publication Data
Siino, Betsy Sikora.
  What your rabbit needs / Betsy Sikora Siino.-- 1st American ed.
      p. cm. -- (What your pet needs)
Includes index.
  ISBN 0-7894-6312-1
  1. Rabbits. I. Title. II. Series.
  SF453 .S55 2000
  636.9'322--dc21
  00-008283

See our complete catalog at
www.dk.com